HAWKS, OWLS & OTHER
Birds of Prey

TEXT
Denise K. Fourie

SERIES EDITOR
Vicki León

PHOTOGRAPHS
Frank Balthis, Denver Bryan, Hal Clason, Jeff Foott,
John Fowler, François Gohier, Phyllis Greenberg, Richard Hansen,
Frans Lanting, Tom Mangelsen, Dennis Sheridan, W.E. Townsend, Jr.

DESIGN
Ashala Nicols-Lawler

MAPS
Cathi Von Schimmelmann

TOOLS AND WEAPONS: *Sharply hooked beaks and powerful talons or claws mark all birds of prey except vultures and condors. Their beaks and feet are not designed for killing, so they must wait for other animals to die and decay before dining. The red-tailed hawk (large photo) uses its weapons to grab and knock out prey. Bald eagles love salmon. Their agile talons (small photo) are well adapted for stealing fish from other birds also. The osprey, on the other hand, really works at fishing. Osprey talons have "anti-skid" pads to hold slippery fishes. Owls and many varieties of eagles often have feathers right down to their talons.*

What are BIRDS of PREY?

Someone mentions birds of prey, and you think of grace at a distance, huge birds that soar and circle with wings outstretched to catch the invisible heat of the thermal winds, slowly sky-writing their signatures across the infinite blue.

They may look carefree, but these avian hunters mean business. As a group, these birds range from the jay-sized American kestrel to the 7 1/2-foot wing span of the bald eagle. They all share the ability to see keenly, stalk patiently, strike swiftly, and kill deftly.

Also called raptors, birds of prey hunt in a variety of ways. Ospreys dive below the surface of the water to snatch fish. Owls and hawks swoop from high perches, or boldly stalk gophers face-to-face in a field. Power diving at up to 200 mph, peregrine falcons knock smaller birds dead in midair. Vultures and condors, on the other hand, spot their dinners from aloft and saunter up on foot. Because their prey is already dead, they have no need for the fierce talons or claws possessed by other raptors. When times are lean, bald eagles and other birds of prey also add carrion or dead animals to their diet.

Young or adult, birds of prey have big appetites which demand almost non-stop hunting. For instance, six baby barn owls and their parents will eat nearly 1,000 rodents

and other small mammals in just one breeding season. A bounty of two dozen mice – with a rattler thrown in for good measure – is all in a day's work for a red-tailed hawk. Peregrine falcons average one plump pigeon per day. Great horned owls consume animals as large and as unpromising as skunks.

Which birds make up this group of skillful predators? Member families include the owl, osprey, falcon, vulture, and hawk. (Biologists classify eagles as part of the hawk family.) Because they eat animals, birds, or fish almost exclusively, birds of prey occupy a special niche in the food chain of the world. Their carnivorous diet plays a key role in the balance of nature.  By keeping rodent populations under control, raptors help farmers and by extension, all humans. By eating dead animals, raptors also help prevent the spread of disease.

Raptor hunting patterns differ according to the hours they keep. Eagles, hawks, falcons, and kites are diurnal hunters, awake and stalking their kill during daylight hours. Owls, on the other hand, are primarily nocturnal creatures. Relying on their keen senses of vision and hearing, they swoop out of the dark onto unsuspecting rabbits, squirrels, and opossums, silent as moths but far more deadly.

Found worldwide, birds of prey thrive in diverse habitats. Most frequently seen throughout North America is the adaptable red-tailed hawk. It is as much at home nesting in the cactus of the Southwestern deserts as it is in lush Eastern woodlands. Bald eagles often summer near the icy, salmon-filled rivers of Alaska and Canada, flying south to winter in Florida, Texas, and California. Many varieties of hawks and owls prefer the rich farmlands of the Midwest and the wide-open prairies of the West, where they can easily spot dinner at a distance. Osprey favor watery locales such as the tranquil barrier islands off the Atlantic and Gulf Coasts. The regal peregrine falcon and other raptors even live on

skyscrapers and in abandoned buildings in many cities and towns. The only places you're unlikely to find raptors are oceanic islands and polar areas where there are no food sources to support the birds. In this book, we'll be focusing our binoculars on many fascinating examples of the 55 raptor species native to North America.

Like other species in today's world, these magnificent hunters themselves fall prey to the increasing, often negative impact of mankind. Loss of habitat due to human development has endangered several species of owls, hawks, and falcons. It has also resulted in the near demise of the California condor. These huge vultures formerly ranged from British Columbia to Baja California. Today, only a handful remain alive in zoos. Fish-eating osprey and bald eagles have also suffered from the presence of pesticides in rivers and lakes. Toxic chemicals absorbed by the fish are passed along the food chain, causing death and infertility to the birds. Peregrine falcons have been similarly threatened.

About six raptors now appear on the Federal Endangered Species list. Dozens more continue to be threatened. Official protection, captive breeding strategies, and other measures are being taken to reverse this downward population spiral. But the best weapon for saving these fierce but fragile hunters in our skies is public education. People need to know what raptors do, and what they do for us. Besides their extraordinary utility in controlling rodents and ridding the earth of decaying animal matter, raptors give us special intangibles. They exemplify beauty, power, majesty. In them, we see and exult in a wild freedom we can never know.

Magnificent even from their downy infancy (pictured bottom left), golden eagles get their name from the metallic shine of their head and neck feathers. Somewhat smaller than the bald eagle, the golden is a tireless hunter, needing 350 pounds of food per year to live.

Long accused of carrying off sheep and other livestock, the golden actually concentrates on rabbits. It also enthusiastically devours any carrion or dead animals it finds, which may have given rise to these tales.

The golden eagle's preferred manmade perch is the utility pole, an unfortunate choice since the bird is sometimes electrocuted when its wings touch high-voltage wires. Utility companies, working with raptor conservation groups, have been redesigning power lines to prevent these unnecessary deaths, as our picture shows.

Summer Range

Winter Range

All Year

Spring & Fall Migration

RAPTOR REAL ESTATE: *Bald and golden eagles are master nest-builders. Their huge aeries, hundreds of pounds of sticks, moss, and branches, need tall sturdy trees to hold them. Some nests are centuries old. Osprey, kestrels, and falcons often prefer less elaborate nests on manmade sites, from skyscrapers to NASA towers. Owls tend to borrow nests or use caves, barns, and burrows.*

Bald
EAGLES

Perhaps the raptor we most readily recognize is the bald eagle. With its snowy head, piercing eyes, dark body plumage, and brilliant yellow beak and talons, this fish-eating member of the hawk family presents an imposing sight along forested waterways.

Don't be misled by the name – this eagle is anything but bald. The term survives from Old English: *balde* means white-headed. The dapper white head and tail feathers don't appear until breeding age at four to five years. They transform the motley brown teenage bird into a stylish adult *Halaeetus leucocephalus*.

The immature bald eagle is often mistaken for its tawny cousin, the golden eagle, but their diets and habitat are quite different. The golden eagle ranges over open fields and canyons to hunt rabbits and rodents. The bald eagle is most at home in estuaries, rivers, lakes – wherever the fishing is good! These birds do share extraordinary visual powers. They can spot mouse-sized prey up to two miles away.

Like most birds of prey, the female bald eagle is larger than the male. The size of a large housecat, she measures up to 45 inches in height and weighs up to 14 pounds. Although the bald eagle prefers to dine on fish, it also feeds on waterfowl, garbage, and road-killed animals. This last diet

item occasionally proves fatal, when the eagles themselves become victims of swift-moving cars.

In 1782, the Continental Congress of the newly formed United States wrangled over the selection of a national symbol. Political leader Ben Franklin hotly contested the choice of the bald eagle (his vote was for the turkey) because of what he called its "bad moral character." Franklin was referring to the eagle's penchant for piracy: stealing food from other birds. A favorite trick is to dive-bomb an osprey in flight. As the osprey grips a freshly-caught salmon, the eagle forces it to drop its catch. The thief speeds after the fallen fish and neatly intercepts it before splashdown.

Bald eagles in the wild can live to be over 20 years old and tend to mate for life. Their nests – called aeries – are huge structures, "remodeled" annually with additions of sticks, branches, feathers, and moss. Some reach nine feet

Bald eagles are famous for airshows more exciting than any barnstorming biplane: whistling climbs, thunderbolt dives, freefall cartwheels. Sometimes two eagles will lock talons and spin through the blue together. Courtship and territorial rivalry are thought to be the motives behind these aerial pyrotechnics.

Bald eagles have plenty of time for such behavior. Their skill as predators and their relatively modest food requirements means they only need spend several hours a day hunting. Rather than hunt, this raptor often prefers to steal another bird's catch (photo at lower left). Seventy percent of a bald eagle's diet is fish; the rest consists of rodents, ducks, and carrion. More social than golden eagles, bald eagles congregate where fishing is especially good. In locales like the Chilkat River Valley in Alaska, where chum salmon spawn each year, eagles can glut themselves with little effort.

across. Bald eagles have quite particular requirements for successful breeding: solitude, protection from humans, large and mature trees to house their nests, and access to water for hunting.

Breeding bald eagle pairs produce an average of two eggs every spring. During 35 days of incubation, the eggs or clutch are closely guarded from raccoons and other prowlers. Mother and father share parenting chores: nest-sitting, hunting, feeding. Once hatched, the fight for survival remains intense. Only half the eaglets survive the first year. Danger takes many forms – including sibling rivalry. Stronger eaglets often kill and eat a weaker sibling.

A s comfortable in Alaskan snow as in the pine and palmetto woods of Florida, bald eagles think nothing of migrating 3,000 miles at a time. Small groups of breeding pairs can be found almost everywhere there is good fishing, from the Rio Verde River in Arizona to the Snake River Canyon in Idaho. Big but incredibly light, thanks to hollow bones and featherlight feathers, these raptors have lots of power in reserve.

Chicks stay in the massive nests for ten weeks or so. At four years and after several molts, they grow their bold adult plumage.

My favorite place to view bald eagles is the Puget Sound area of the Pacific Northwest. Canoeing in a quiet bay off Vancouver Island, we have often watched as a pair of bald eagles fished for their breakfast. White feathers glinting in the morning sun, they perch like sentinels in the tall pines, perennially on the alert for a weakened salmon or an injured duck.

In such a pristine setting, it's easy to forget this raptor's plight. Before 1800, biologists guess that bald eagles numbered as many as 75,000 in the continental United States. By 1970, the count had dipped to a precarious 3,000. Why the drastic decline? A variety of perils: egg collectors, irresponsible hunters, loss of habitat, pesticide contamination, and more. The landmark Bald Eagle Protection Act of 1940 made the killing, possession, or selling of the bird or its parts illegal. Bald eagles were given further protection in 1969 and added to the Federal Endangered Species list. Killing a bald eagle today means a steep fine and a jail term.

Thanks to these laws, the U.S. Fish and Wildlife Service estimates there may now be 5,000 bald eagles in the lower 48 states. Alaska remains the bald eagle stronghold, with about 50,000 birds.

It's too early to relax. Bald eagles continue to be endangered in 43 of the lower 48 states. Despite laws, ranchers continue to shoot or poison eagles, supposedly to prevent livestock loss. And death by electrocution on power lines remains common.

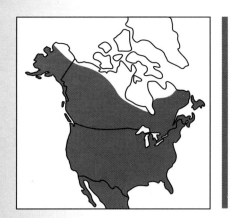

All Year

Great Horned OWLS

Startled out of a sound sleep, you bolt upright in your bed or sleeping bag. What was that eerie cry that sent shivers down your spine? It's the unmistakable, mournful call of the great horned owl, echoing through the night.

Equally at home in the suburbs or the wilderness, North America's most common owl is found in back yards, orchards, and city parks as well as in forest, desert, and chaparral habitats. Largest of the "eared" owls, the great horned owl (*Bubo virginianus*) ranges from the Canadian tundra line through the United States and to the tip of South America. Enormous yellow eyes and a large head give it a droll, all-knowing appearance. Its two-foot height and wingspan of up to five feet also can present an intimidating air.

An aggressive hunter, the great horned owl eats just about anything that moves. Cottontail rabbits make up about half of its diet, but the menu includes mice, chipmunks, snakes, gophers, frogs, robins, sparrows, and bats. Even the pungent smell doesn't deter this voracious raptor from munching skunks. As a result, owl nests and bodies smell breathtaking in the very worst sense of the word. Red-tailed hawks and smaller owls also fall prey to

this bold raptor, as well as animals that outweigh it, including opossums and housecats.

The great horned owl prefers to sleep during the day, staying hidden in treetops. As darkness falls, the drowsy owl becomes an alert and hungry hunter, scanning the ground from its perch or patrolling the territory on powerful wings. Very soft plumage and special serrated edges on the primary wing feathers make the great horned owl's flight silent and doubly deadly. Occasionally, flocks of smaller birds – usually crows, jays, or blackbirds – get their revenge by mobbing the owl as it naps. Annoyed by their aggression, the owl finally leaves its roost to seek quieter quarters.

The tufted 2-inch high "ears" giving the owl its horned look are clumps of feathers used in threat displays. Look for the real ears as asymmetrically placed cavities on either side of the head. Each ear perceives auditory clues differently, helping the owl pinpoint the location and height of a sound. This remarkable sense of hearing, coupled with keen vision, make nighttime hunting possible. Contrary to folklore, an owl sees best in broad daylight, and sometimes

Great horned owls begin life as downy chicks (center photo); by two months, they take on the characteristic facial feathering of the adult (far left) but lack ear tufts. Although the tufted "ears" are there to threaten, they don't seem to do the job. Birds half this owl's size often harass it in the daytime, when they know the great horned owl is trying to catch a siesta and not its dinner.

A roll call of owls found across the U.S. and Canada includes, left to right: the barn owl; a startled long-eared owl juvenile; a screech owl; and an immature great gray owl. The latter is now rare in the mountain portion of its range, and the barn owl has endangered status in several states.

hunts then. Because its eyes are fixed in their sockets, the owl must rotate its head to change views. Sounds painful, but it's easily accomplished with a flexible, thick neck that turns 270 degrees – three-quarters of a circle.

For the Greeks and others, the owl symbolized wisdom. Legends aside, the owl is not as scholarly as it looks. Unlike falcons and other raptors, owls do not respond well to human training.

For bird watchers, the great horned owl can be a relatively easy bird to track. Gray or brown, oblong "pellets" – indigestible clumps of regurgitated fur, bones, feathers, skulls scattered beneath their roost – are a telltale sign. Unlike hawks, owls tend to swallow their prey whole or in large chunks, bones and all.

More advice for would-be owl watchers: track pellets by day, hooting by night, then canvas the neighborhood for a large, cat-like outline in the fork of a tree. Try mimicking

the hooting call. Chances are good you'll get a response.

The great horned owl has a distant cousin which is North America's second most widespread owl species: the barn owl. With its heart-shaped facial disk and dark, sunken eyes, the barn owl presents a ghostly figure, flitting from deserted buildings or trees to kill a dozen mice each night. More southerly in range than the great horned owl, it prefers open grassland and farmland for hunting rodents. The most widely distributed bird in the world, the barn owl nevertheless is losing ground. Their numbers have fallen most sharply in the American Midwest, where agricultural land and barns to nest in are getting scarcer.

On the other hand, the great horned owl seems to hold its own despite human encroachment. Its diverse eating habits, versatile hunting techniques, and ability to live anywhere from an arid canyon to a snowy forest let this bird coexist with humans and wilderness alike.

Owl mating rituals are rarely seen but are fascinating. Great horned owl couples bow to one another, stroke each other, and touch beaks. Finally the male pays the female the compliment of a dead mouse laid at her feet, which she accepts or rejects.

Summer Range

All Year

BIRDS OF A FEATHER: *Raptors molt or shed feathers annually. Plumage varies with age, sex, and climate, giving birds of the same species a very different look. Young raptors go through a fuzzy stage and several molts before getting their final set of plumes. All this makes it tough for birders to firmly identify species. A young bald eagle tends to look much like a golden eagle, for instance. Red-tailed hawks can differ from bird to bird, and from region to region.*

Red-tailed HAWKS

While the great horned owl oversees the woods and fields by night, the red-tailed hawk works the day shift over much of the same terrain. Perched on telephone poles and tree snags throughout the United States, you often see the chunky body, fan-shaped tail and rounded wings of this diurnal soaring hawk.

Buteos, eagles, accipiters, and kites make up the large, diverse hawk family. How can you tell them apart? Watch them in flight. Buteos or soaring hawks have thicker wings and broader tails. The red-tailed hawk and other buteos soar for hours on afternoon updrafts of warm air called thermals as they seek out rodents in the open fields.

Eagles are best distinguished by their huge size and long wings. Accipiters like the goshawk and sharp-shinned hawk are known as bird hawks because smaller birds form the mainstay of their diet. Shorter wings and longer tails give them the speed and agility needed to catch their prey on the wing and in the brush. The graceful kites have long, slim tails and pointed wings.

Widespread from the tundra line to Central America, the red-tailed hawk varies in color, depending on age and subspecies. Typically, an adult red-tail has dark bands midway down its white belly and a distinctive tail, shining like a copper penny against the sun.

Splendid soaring creatures,
echo of Icarus,
successor to pterodactyls,
when you lift your great bodies into the air
our hearts
become airborne also

Another raptor that loves to roost on power poles, the red-tailed hawk loses many of its number to electrocution each year.

The red-tail is part of the big buteo or soaring hawk family. Buteos have broad wings and large, fan-shaped tails. Other buteo beauties include Swainson's hawk and Harris' hawk. Accipiters or bird hawks have long thin tails and shorter wings. These agile woodland hawks include the goshawk and the sharp-shinned hawk.

Whether you are hiking the coastal foothills of Southern California or the ridges of Appalachia, the red-tailed hawk frequently appears as an aerial companion. As it circles overhead, its raspy "kreeee" pierces the air.

Annual migration occurs mainly among the northern subspecies. From September to November, birders gather at Hawk Mountain Sanctuary in eastern Pennsylvania to witness spectacular displays of migrating raptors. Each year, about 5,000 red-tailed hawks pass overhead enroute to southern wintering grounds. These magnificent gatherings are called "kettles."

Raucous in courtship, red-tails scream, dive-bomb, and grapple before settling down to domestic life. They lay their clutch of two to three eggs in a sturdy nest of twigs, bark, and evergreen boughs. Red-tails are often two-nest families, using alternate sites in a given neighborhood over the years. Owls often appropriate their abandoned nests, preferring to borrow rather than build.

A nest with a view is the preference of red-tails. This can mean a home high in the fork of the tallest tree on the wood's edge. In the desert, hawk families nest on cliff ledges and in saguaro cactuses.

The versatile red-tail can hunt while soaring and from a perching position. At the sight of prey, the hawk plunges earthward. At times approaching race-car speeds of 120 mph, the bird sinks its talons into the back or neck of its victim. With larger prey such as snakes or weasels, the animal may still be alive when carried off in flight. This often provokes a spectacular aerial fight to the finish between hunter and

NATIONAL
WILDLIFE
REFUGE

UNAUTHORIZED ENTRY
PROHIBITED

U. S. DEPARTMENT OF THE INTERIOR
FISH AND WILDLIFE SERVICE

prey. Rattlesnakes, a favorite food of desert subspecies, have been known to inflict their fatal bite in midair on red-tails.

For years, farmers have unfairly maligned *Buteo jamaicens* as a chicken-eating machine. Although individual birds occasionally snatch a chicken, red-tail hawks feed on rodents about 85% of the time. Like the great horned owl, it supplements that diet with other small mammals, birds, reptiles, and insects.

Despite legal protection, the shooting of hawks for suspected poultry predation continues. Interestingly, studies of the contents of hawks' stomachs now show that this raptor is vital in keeping rat, mice, and rabbit populations under control. When red-tailed hawk populations are reduced by hunting, the resultant explosion of rodents decimates farm crops.

Quite a number of hawks, including the red-tailed hawk, migrate in the spring and/or the fall. Flying in large groups called "kettles," they present a stirring sight as they pass over certain favored observation spots each year.

Both the north and south shores of the Great Lakes region see large hawk migrations in March-April and September-October. In New Jersey, Cape May is a vantage point for osprey, falcon, and hawk migration each fall. Hawk Mountain Sanctuary near Kempton, Pennsylvania, has spring and fall hawk-watching in great numbers. Point Diablo in Northern California sees great masses of kites and hawks August through October. Even the urban parks of New York City offer good viewing of hawks from Canada, migrating south each fall.

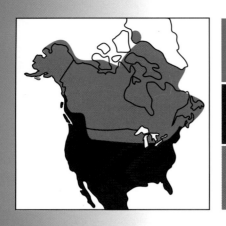

Summer Range

Winter Range

Spring & Fall Migration

AERIAL ACROBATS: *Many birds of prey besides the peregrine falcon are speedsters. The bald eagle dives at 60 mph. Prairie falcons can outfly their peregrine cousins at times. Even condors soar at speeds of 50 mph or more. Raptor agility is legendary too, from the low swift glide of the harrier to the black-and-white grace of the swallow-tailed kite.*

Peregrine
FALCONS

*I*f peregrine falcons were motorists, they would collect speeding tickets like nobody's business. *Falco peregrinus*, the world's fastest bird, cruises along at 75 mph just in normal flight. When it accelerates into its hunting dive, radar guns have clocked the bird at over 200 mph. That makes it the fastest creature on earth, period.

A sleek design enables the falcon to zip through the air at high speeds. Smaller than a red-tailed hawk, this two-to three-pound raptor is equipped with a narrow tail and long tapered wings that fold back to decrease air resistance. Blue-gray above, cream-colored chest below, the peregrine sports a dark hood and facial markings aptly termed a "mustache."

Peregrines have a fascinating hunting style. They cruise along, 1,000 feet above the earth, scanning for pigeons or other birds. When they sight a likely victim, peregrines go into a "stoop" or dive, hitting their prey at full tilt with their large feet, often tearing the flesh. As the paralyzed quarry tumbles earthward, the peregrine nips below to catch it on the way down.

Nicknamed "duck hawk," the peregrine actually prefers smaller birds. Pigeons, mourning doves, swifts, swallows, robins, and murrelets are standard fare. Peregrines depend on available food sources for their diet, sometimes lunching

on pintail duck, other times snacking on migrating Monarch butterflies.

Famous for its aerial prowess, the peregrine has been a newsmaker in recent years for other, sadder reasons. Between 1950 and 1965, the number of peregrine falcons worldwide dramatically declined. On its diet of insect-eating birds, the peregrine was getting massive doses of pesticides. DDT, PCBs, and other chemicals passed through the food chain, concentrating in the falcons. Their brick-red eggs became calcium deficient. Shells were so thin that they cracked under the weight of the mother bird. By the early 1970s, only 30 known breeding pairs remained in the United States.

In 1970, Cornell University pioneered a captive breeding program to save these raptors. Known as the Peregrine Fund and now located at the World Center for Birds of Prey in Idaho, the program has released over 2,600 peregrine falcons into wild and urban settings. One of Cornell's most successful strategies has been to take eggs from wild peregrines' nests and substitute dummy eggs. The real eggs are then hatched in laboratories, and the new chicks are returned to the wild and placed in the nests where the dummy eggs were.

Another strategy to improve survival has been the introduction of peregrines into urban settings. Peregrine natural habitat consists of open country with high, rocky cliffs for nesting and a commanding view for hunting. To nest, the parents merely scrape out a small hollow in the

gravel on top of a bluff. City skyscrapers are remarkably similar to these steep ledges. And nesting on man-made structures is not new. For millenia, falcons have lived on the Egyptian pyramids and on castle turrets and church towers throughout Europe.

With plenty of pigeons nearby as prey, the only improvement needed to make a high-rise a home has been the installation of gravel-filled nesting boxes. Breeding peregrines now reside on top of office buildings in many North American cities, including Montreal, Washington, Los Angeles, and Boston. With few predators to eat the young, the peregrines' only problem in the city has been a tendency to crash into windows.

As peregrines are restored to new and traditional locations, nature lovers and urban dwellers alike can delight in the spiraling courtship displays of this speed demon. Prior to mating, the male falcon performs a spectacular dive similar to the hunting stoop, complete with screams and ritual feeding of his mate.

The recovery of the peregrine falcon from near extinction has been remarkable. But the bird still faces dangers of several sorts. Its legendary speed and hunting ability make the peregrine much coveted by bonafide falconers and by smugglers who sell the birds in the Middle East and elsewhere for large sums. DDT remains a problem also. Now outlawed in Canada and the U.S., the pesticide is still heavily used in Mexico and South America. It works its way through the food chain from insects to small birds to the peregrine, causing infertility and death.

Falconry, or the art of training falcons, hawks, and other birds to hunt for man, has been popular for millenia. Once the sport of kings and nobles, falconry is now the province of those affluent enough to pay prices that can be in the high five-figure range for a peregrine falcon. Other raptors, such as kestrels, goshawks and red-tailed hawks, command less exalted prices.

About 2,500 licensed falconers live in the U.S., their activities strictly controlled by the U.S. Fish and Wildlife Service. To keep bird populations in balance, only a limited number of peregrines and other birds may be used for falconry.

Pictured at left: a California falconer puts a hood on his peregrine falcon, a device which keeps the bird calm while traveling.

Pictured above: peregrines have been found to thrive not just in wild settings but on tall buildings in the "urban jungle" as well.

**FOOD CAN BE
FATAL:** *Raptors
today eat what they
always have. But
much of their
diet – fish, rodents,
other birds – is
riddled with DDT,
lead, and other
toxins causing
infertility and
death. The virtual
extinction of the
California condor is
sad proof that "you
are what you eat."
Unlike humans,
raptors cannot shop
elsewhere for
pesticide-free food.*

California
CONDORS

Averaging 20-odd pounds and darkening the sky with a 10-foot wingspan, the California condor reigns as North America's largest flying land bird. "Reigns" is unfortunately the wrong word. Now officially extinct in the wild, the condor's kingdom has been reduced to about 30 birds held in captivity. The pitiful remnants of this prehistoric species were rounded up in 1986 and 1987 from their remote stronghold near Santa Barbara. Helicopters lifted the condor cargo to specially prepared "condorminiums" at the Los Angeles Zoo and the San Diego Wild Animal Park. There they are being studied, and a captive breeding program is underway in a controversial last-ditch effort to save the species.

As far as looks go, the condor will never win any beauty contests. Pinkish-red, crinkly skin covers its large, naked, red-eyed head. A spiked ruff of black feathers ring the gawky neck. The rest of the bulky body is covered in black plumage except for white "underarms." When viewed from below, these triangle-shaped wing patches help identify the condor.

Baldness is a characteristic common to all vultures, the name given to this entire family of carrion-eating birds. Bacteria often infest the carcasses they feed on. By eliminating head feathers, bacteria lack a convenient place

to grow. Although termed birds of prey, the California condor and other vultures differ from hawks, owls, falcons, and osprey, all true hunters. Condors do not kill prey. As scavengers, they forage for fresh carcasses. Dead deer, cattle, and sheep are their favorite foods.

To feed, condors insert their heads into body cavities or wounds. Although this may seem like a highly repulsive action, it is of value. By eating dead animals, condors and their kin curtail the spread of harmful bacteria.

Condors have lived in North America for at least 10,000 years. Fossil remains in the Grand Canyon show that early condors fed on the carcasses of mammoths, camels, and saber-toothed tigers, all long extinct in North America. Condors probably ranged from the Pacific Coast across the U.S. to Florida. After the last Ice Age, the reduction of large herds of grazing animals brought the heyday of the condor to an end.

Much later, in the 19th and 20th centuries, human expansion across North America put the final crunch on the condors. Since Gold Rush days, their numbers have been

critically low. Always a target for hunters, condors were pushed to extinction by growing demand on rangeland, ingestion of lead buckshot and other heavy metals, air pollution, loss of habitat, and an influx of humans into breeding areas. All these factors have had detrimental effects on the skittish birds.

The condor's own reproductive cycle has worked against the survival of the species. It takes about five to seven years for *Gymnogyps Californianus* to reach breeding age. Clutch size is always one egg. Raising a chick takes almost two years, so the parents only breed every other year. Female condors are able to "double clutch," that is, to lay a second egg during the breeding season in case something happens to the first. Here is where scientists have intervened to fool Mother Nature. Beginning in 1979, ornithologists climbed to the cave-nests of the last free-breeding condor pairs, and carefully removed their eggs. These eggs were placed in incubators. If second eggs were laid, they were also removed. A dozen wild condor eggs have been successfully hatched in the zoos. These young birds are now the nucleus of the captive breeding program.

Opponents of this recovery program warned that the finicky condors would refuse to breed in zoos. Not so. April 27, 1988, saw the birth of Molloko – the first

California condor conceived and hatched in captivity.

Molloko, like all zoo-hatched condor chicks, was fed a diet of regurgitated mice by a trainer using a condor hand puppet. The chicks imprint on the image of a condor rather than the face of a human, thus keeping the animals in a state as close as possible to the wild one.

The Condor Recovery Project, jointly sponsored by the California Fish and Game Commission and the U.S. Fish and Wildlife Service, aims to "reestablish a free-living, self-sustaining population of condors in California" by the mid-1990s. Costing over $20 million to date, the recovery efforts have employed such techniques as releasing Andean condors, the closest living relative of the California condor, into the Los Padres National Forest for study. Biologists are using the more numerous Andean species as a surrogate group to gain as much knowledge as possible before releasing California condors into the wild.

Meanwhile, the California condors at the San Diego Wild Animal Park and the Los Angeles Zoo remain out of the public eye. Until it is determined that the population is stable and growing, these condors – the ungainly hope for the future – will continue to live and breed in unstressed seclusion.

The most common carrion eater in North and South America, the turkey vulture is easily identified by its naked red head and its soaring style. Often seen in groups, turkey vultures cruise in circles, their wings tilted up to form a V. The vulture pictured on this page lives in Texas. Vultures, are found worldwide, including Africa.

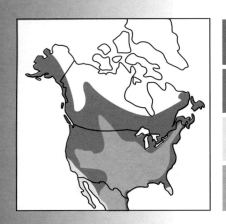

Summer Range

Winter Range

All Year

Spring & Fall Migration

SOUND EFFECTS:
The osprey may be the most musical sounding bird of prey, whistling loudly while it works. Owls produce a whole range of spooky night noises: hoots, whistles, shrieks, and moans. A harsh "kee-kee" identifies the golden eagle. His cousin the bald eagle makes a softer echo. Red-tailed hawks utter a high-pitched "kreeee" while soaring. When excited, vultures simply hiss.

OSPREY

When it comes to fishing, the osprey is the envy of human anglers. This remarkable fish-eating bird of prey doesn't need fancy rods, reels, or bait to catch a big one. The osprey uses its feet to pluck live trout, flounder, or salmon from the water.

As it glides overhead, the white-breasted osprey resembles a gull. Once its riveting aerial performance begins, the difference is clear. Spying a school of fish in the river below, this large raptor stops short and hurls itself towards the water, reaching speeds of 40 mph. Head and powerful feet extended, it crashes full-force into the water.

Usually the osprey surfaces with a wiggling fish. In a flash the raptor is airborne again, pausing briefly to shake off excess water like a puppy after a swim. It also aligns the fish headfirst to reduce air resistance in flight.

As a fisherman, the osprey has adaptations that set it apart from other diurnal raptors. Talons are curved and sharp like meat hooks. Special nonskid pads known as "spicules" cover the bottom of each toe to prevent slippery fish from sliding away. Like owls, the osprey has one reversible talon. Two strong talons on either side let it hold prey tightly.

Oily, compact feathers keep the bird well-insulated and streamline the body for diving. Although nicknamed

"fish hawk" or "sea eagle," the osprey is in a separate family from true hawks.

Where does *Pandion haliaetus* live? Along seacoasts and near large bodies of fresh water. Next to the barn owl, the osprey is the most widely distributed bird on the globe. In the United States, the largest colony — some 1,600 breeding pairs — resides in Chesapeake Bay, Maryland.

As with other raptors, the pesticide DDT caused thinning in osprey eggshells. During the 1950s and 1960s, broken eggs and alarmingly low reproductive rates were common. With the DDT ban in 1972 and renewed attention to our ecosystem, the North American osprey population is staging a cautious comeback.

The osprey makes an impressively handsome picture. Measuring six feet with wings spread, it is nearly as large as a bald eagle. Its golden eyes are emphasized by bold, black eyeliner markings. White underparts contrast with dark brown wings and a

If it looks like fowl play, it is. Many raptors have elaborate aerial courtship rituals, and the osprey is no exception. Mating itself is a pretty standard affair, the male hopping onto the female's back for a brief interval.

Coast-loving osprey populations often mate, nest, and rear young in Mexico, Central America, and other southern locales. Although its range is world-wide, the osprey remains uncommon almost everywhere.

speckled head. Even the eggs are strikingly colored: maroon blotches on a vanilla-white background.

Each winter, North American osprey migrate south to the tropics. Unable to dive-bomb through frozen surfaces, they must leave the icy fishing grounds of the north in order to survive. Spring finds them homing in on familiar breeding grounds and sprucing up last year's nest.

These huge, 700- to 800- pound nests, typically located on cliffs or in dead trees with commanding ocean or river views, also serve as hunting platforms. During the breeding season, the male bird works overtime from this base to feed his family. His ravenous brood can devour seven pounds of fish a day.

Less abundant than in times past, osprey can still be spotted by birders in the know. Prime osprey habitats include Baja California, the barrier islands of the Atlantic and Gulf Coasts, the Florida coast, the Great Lakes, and the waterways of the Pacific Northwest. Not surprisingly, this aquatic hunter also thrives wherever there are fish hatcheries!

Since human history began, birds of prey have figured as symbols and myths. Falcons once nested in the pyramids of Egypt, and were worshipped as the sun god Horus. The ancient Greeks associated the owl with wisdom and made it the sacred bird of Athena. Along the Pacific Coast, Chumash Indians once sacrificed condors in religious rituals. Many Native American tribes revered the eagle, using its feathers to indicate rank. Long associated with strength and military might, eagles and hawks have served as national symbols for countries as diverse as the U.S., Russia, Mexico, and Austria.

As the world has grown more crowded with humans, admiration has often turned to exploitation and competition. Raptor species continue to shrink because of illegal collecting, shooting, pesticides, and electrocution. But the toughest problem remains habitat loss. Birds of prey need lots of room. A typical square mile of desert supports 18,000 mice and 100 quail. That same area supports just two great horned owls and two red-tailed hawks. The work of groups like the Nature Conservancy, which buys large land tracts to be held as wilderness, offers perhaps the raptors' best hope.

There are other bright spots. For example, Audubon members now keep a closer watch on local breeding patterns and habitat loss. As a decline is documented, species get placed on the Audubon Blue List. This identifies troubled bird species at a much earlier stage than the extremes required for the Federal Threatened and Endangered Species list.

People are also working with captive birds. Centers across the U.S. rescue and rehabilitate birds, do research, carry out captive breeding programs, and put on events and educational demonstrations.

Today's zoos and wildlife parks also build habitats for raptors that closely resemble their home in the wild. This is not only more interesting and humane, it's more educational. Visitors learn that habitats are as varied and complex as city neighborhoods, and infinitely more fragile. Zoos and parks of all sorts give us a look at living things we would otherwise never see. Zoos would be the first to insist, however, that our primary responsibility is to preserve the native habitats of these same living things.

Even if we did not value the beauty and grace of raptors, we cannot ignore them. Because of their almost unlimited mobility and their position at the top of the food chain, birds of prey act as an early warning system for the health of the entire planet. In their fate is written our own.

The effects of DDT and other chemicals are clear. The discolored, thin-shelled egg at left comes from a bird whose diet is tainted with pesticides. Even though DDT is now forbidden in the U.S., raptors such as the osprey (pictured at right on Mexican cactus) migrate south and eat chemical-laden food there.

ACKNOWLEDGMENTS

PHOTOGRAPHERS:

Frank Balthis: page 22, top; page 34, bottom
Denver Bryan/Comstock Inc.: back cover portrait of a juvenile great horned owl
Hal Clason: pages 20-21
Jeff Foott: page 3, bottom; page 4, top; page 5; page 9; page 10, top; page 17, right; pages 30-31; page 40; inside back cover
John Fowler: page 8, bottom; page 10, bottom
François Gohier: page 29; page 34, top; page 37
Phyllis Greenberg/Comstock Inc.: page 7; page 8, top; page 35
Richard Hansen: page 3, top; page 13; page 16, right; page 19; page 23; page 26, top and bottom
Frans Lanting: front cover portrait of a bald eagle; page 11; page 25; page 27; page 33; page 36; pages 38-39
Tom Mangelsen: inside front cover; page 15, right; page 22, bottom

Dennis Sheridan: title page; page 4, bottom; page 14; page 15, left; page 16, left
W.E. Townsend, Jr.: page 17, left

ABOUT THE AUTHOR:

From her home in California's bird-rich midsection, author Denise K. Fourie is well-placed to keep an eye on the birds she writes about. A professional librarian, Denise is also a research consultant and writer specializing in natural and local history topics.

SPECIAL THANKS:

Doug Stinson; Ron Ruppert, Cuesta College; Nancy Marx, U.S. Fish and Wildlife Service; Nancy Bushby, Patuxent Wildlife Research Center; Lisa Langelier, World Center for Birds of Prey; Deborah Pollack and June Bottcher, Los Angeles Zoo; Hawk Mountain Sanctuary; Kevin Buchanan, Montery County Park Ranger.

TO LEARN MORE ABOUT BIRDS OF PREY

Raptor study centers across the U.S. conduct research and breeding programs, present exhibits, and put on educational programs. Among them:
➤ *World Center for Birds of Prey and the Peregrine Fund,* 5666 West Flying Hawk Lane, Boise Idaho 83709; (208) 362-3716.
➤ *Hawk Mountain Sanctuary Association*, Route 2, Kempton, Pennsylvania 19529; (215) 756-6961.

Many zoos across the U.S. and Canada have raptors on display. You can see bald eagles at over 60 zoos, great horned owls at 70. The rare California condor population is confined to the two zoos listed. Neither group is on display at this time, but videos and other exhibits can be seen. You can get a closeup look at Andean condors, however, at the New York Bronx Zoo, the Detroit Zoo, and 28 other zoos.

➤**Los Angeles Zoo,** 5333 Zoo Drive, Los Angeles, California 90027; (213) 666-4650.
➤**San Diego Wild Animal Park**, Highway 78, Escondido, California 92025; (619) 234-6541.
➤Other good raptor displays can be seen at zoos in Portland, Seattle, Phoenix, Birmingham, Atlanta, Dallas, New Orleans, Milwaukee, St. Louis, San Diego, and Colorado Springs.
➤To see raptor migration in the wild, see pages 22-23.

FOR FURTHER INFO:
National Audubon Society, 950 Third Ave., New York, NY 10022; (212) 832-3200.
American Birding Association, P.O. Box 470, Sonoita, Arizona 85637.
Good books to read: ***The Birders Handbook***: *A Field Guide to the Natural History of North America Birds*, by Paul Ehrlich, and published by Simon & Schuster. Also useful is ***National Wildlife Refuges: A Visitor's Guide***, a free map published by the U.S. Fish and Wildlife Service, which shows locations and facilities of National Wildlife Refuges across the U.S.